P E A R L

S U R V I V O R S

Anthology by Dick Jensen

ISBN 0-9656972-2-3
Copyright 2001 Richard K. Jensen
Greenville, South Carolina, USA

First Edition, 2001
Published by First Foundations, Inc.
Travelers Rest, SC 29690

Printed by Faith Printing Co.
Taylors, SC 29687

In Memory of my father

Kenneth Magill Jensen

Who served in the U.S. Navy 1942-44

Dick Jensen holds the U.S. Flag presented to his mother during graveside services for his father, Kenneth M. Jensen

Bulletin!

"We're being raided. This is an emergency announcement. Pearl Harbor is now being attacked. This is an emergency communique from the Hawaiian Defense Headquarters. It's an actual enemy air raid. This is not a maneuver. We're being attacked. It's an air raid."

Radio station announcer
Honolulu, Hawaii
Sunday morning
December 7, 1941

Presenting

Eyewitness accounts from surviving veterans who were at the following locations during the Japanese attack on Pearl Harbor, Hawaii, December 7, 1941.

USS AVOCET

USS CALIFORNIA

Hickam Field

USS HONOLULU

USS MARYLAND

Navy Hospital

USS NEOSHO

USS NEVADA

USS PENNSYLVANIA

Schofield Barracks

USS ST. LOUIS

Waikiki Beach

Wheeler Field

Visualize the action through their eyes, and with them
REMEMBER PEARL HARBOR!

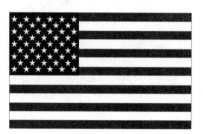

Contents

South Carolina is among the states that honor Pearl Harbor survivors with customized license tags.

How Pearl Harbor looked one month prior to the Japanese attack. Ford Island is in center of picture. *(U.S. Navy photo)*

Pearl Harbor at about 8 a.m. on December 7, 1941. The attack on battleship row is just beginning. Photo taken from Japanese aircraft. Note another Japanese plane to the right of center in photo released by the U.S. Navy after WWII.

Introduction

Pearl Harbor was not about a romantic triangle involving two American fighter pilots in love with the same Navy nurse in Hawaii. That's a *reel* version.

Pearl Harbor *was* about the 2,403 Americans who died violent deaths in a two-hour period on a day that "will live in infamy." That's the *real* version.

In the pages that follow, United States military veterans who escaped that horrible tragedy offer eyewitness accounts of what happened at Pearl Harbor, Hawaii, on December 7, 1941. During the 60th anniversary observance of Japan's surprise aerial attack on the U.S. Navy fleet, more than 7,000 American survivors were still living. The testimonials published here are representative of that group.

It would not have been possible to collect these stories without the assistance of the Pearl Harbor Survivors Association, a national organization that preserves and encourages the study of the historical episodes pertaining to the attack on Pearl Harbor. Many of the veterans profiled in this book are members of PHSA.

Other research led me to previously published stories that were so compelling that I requested permission to have them reproduced in this anthology. My sincere appreciation is extended to those periodicals that granted permission; they are given credit in the text. My gratitude also goes to those who gave permission to use photographs and graphic art. Credits are adjacent to the visual aids.

Some of my findings are based on declassified public information from the Department of Defense. I found the Naval Historical Center in Washington to be a significant source of reliable information, and I recommend its website (www.history.navy.mil) for further study.

Others deserving special recognition are: 1. the Board of Directors of First Foundations, Inc. , the nonprofit organization that commissioned this project; 2. the BI-LO Corporation that agreed to an exclusive distribution of the first printing in their stores in five states; 3. Juanita Barnett of Faith Printing Company; 4. my wife, Marty, who served as principal proofreader of the manuscript and general encourager.

If this little book adds to the understanding of the value of freedom and the sacrifices made to pay freedom's price for posterity, it will have accomplished the author's purpose.

Richard K. "Dick" Jensen
August, 2001

1

Why Pearl Harbor?

A month before the theater release of "Pearl Harbor" — Hollywood's melodramatic treatment of the Japanese attack on Hawaii — this professor surveyed college students about their knowledge of the infamous wake-up call. Some respondents had no clue about the event, others had limited knowledge based on misinformation, and still others offered flippant answers that bordered on disrespect. Overall, the research results were not encouraging for any "Remember Pearl Harbor" advocate.

Why indeed should succeeding generations care about one of the darkest days in the history of the United States? Why should we revisit the scene via the memories of those who were there?

Maybe for reasons comparable to why Jews remember the Holocaust, or why Christians remember the Crucifixion, or why Muslims remember the Crusades. Blood spilled in another era by heroes of a culture is rarely shed in vain — unless the progeny of that culture forget why.

Knowing and interpreting any classic event in history must begin with facts, not fantasy. That sets the movie, "Tora, Tora, Tora," in sharp contrast to the newer movie, "Pearl Harbor." The 1970 film had an all-star cast of both Japanese and American actors who gave a balanced background of the social and political currents that were a prelude to war. "Tora" audiences left theaters with a clearer picture of why Tokyo's torpedoes and bombs slammed into anchored U.S. battleships on a bloody Sunday just before Christmas, 1941.

For the true stories in this book to satisfy more than curiosity, they must be placed in the context of the times. The U. S. Department of Defense provided the following prologue to Pearl.

The road to war between Japan and the United States began in the 1930s when differences over China drove the two nations apart. In 1931, Japan conquered Manchuria, which until then had been part of China. In 1937, Japan began a long and ultimately unsuccessful campaign to conquer the rest of China. In 1940, the Japanese government allied their country with Nazi Germany in the Axis Alliance, and, in the following year, occupied all of Indochina.

The United States, which had important political and economic interests in East Asia, was alarmed by these Japanese moves. The U.S. increased military and financial aid to China, embarked on a program of strengthening its military power in the Pacific, and cut off the shipment of oil and other raw materials to Japan.

Because Japan was poor in natural resources, its government viewed these steps, especially the embargo on oil, as a threat to the nation's survival. Japan's leaders responded by resolving to seize the resource-rich territories on Southeast Asia, even though that move would certainly result in war with the United States.

The problem with the plan was the danger posed by the U.S. Pacific Fleet based at Pearl Harbor. Admiral Isoroku Yamamoto, commander of the Japanese fleet, devised a plan to immobilize the U.S. fleet at the outset of the war with a surprise attack. The key elements in Yamamoto's plans were meticulous preparation, the achievement of surprise, and the use of aircraft carriers and naval aviation on an unprecedented scale. In the spring of 1941, Japanese carrier pilots began training in the special tactics called for by the Pearl Harbor attack plan.

In October 1941, the naval general staff gave final approval to Yamamoto's plan, which called for the formation of an attack force centered around six heavy aircraft carriers accompanied by 24 supporting vessels. A separate group of submarines was to sink any American warships which escaped the Japanese carrier force.

The Japanese fleet assembled in the remote anchorage of Tankan Bay in the Kurile Islands and departed in strictest secrecy for Hawaii on 26 November 1941. The ships' route crossed the North Pacific and avoided normal shipping lanes. At dawn 7 December 1941, the task force had approached undetected to a point slightly more than 200 miles north of Hawaii.

At 6:00 a.m., the six carriers launched a first wave of 181 planes composed of torpedo bombers, dive bombers, horizontal bombers and fighters. Even as they winged south, some elements of U.S. forces on Oahu realized there was something different about this Sunday morning.

In the hours before dawn, U.S. Navy vessels spotted an unidentified submarine periscope near the entrance to Pearl Harbor. It was attacked and reported sunk by the destroyer USS WARD and a patrol plane. At 7:00 a.m., an alert operator of an Army radar station at Opana spotted the approach-

ing first wave of the attack force. The officers to whom
those reports were relayed did not consider them significant
enough to take action. The report of the submarine sinking
was handled routinely, and the radar sighting was passed
off as an approaching group of American planes due to arrive that morning.

The Japanese aircrews achieved complete surprise when
they hit American ships and military installations on Oahu
shortly before 8:00 a.m. They attacked military airfields at
the same time they hit the fleet anchored in Pearl Harbor.
The Navy air bases at Ford Island and Kaneohe Bay, the
Marine airfield at Ewa and the Army Air Corps fields at
Bellows, Wheeler and Hickam were all bombed and strafed
as other elements of the attacking force began their assaults
on the ships moored in Pearl Harbor. The purpose of the
simultaneous attacks was to destroy the American planes
before they could rise to intercept the Japanese.

Of the more than 90 ships at anchor in Pearl Harbor, the
primary targets were the eight battleships anchored there,
seven were moored on Battleship Row along the southeast
shore of Ford Island while the USS PENNSYLVANIA lay
in drydock across the channel. Within the first minutes of
the attack all the battleships adjacent to Ford Island had taken
bomb and or torpedo hits. The USS WEST VIRGINIA sank
quickly. The USS OKLAHOMA turned turtle and sank. At
about 8:10 a.m., the USS ARIZONA was mortally wounded
by an armor-piercing bomb which ignited the ship's forward
ammunition magazine. The resulting explosion and fire
killed 1,177 crewmen, the greatest loss of life on any ship
that day and about half the total number of Americans killed.
The USS CALIFORNIA, USS MARYLAND, USS TEN-
NESSEE, and USS NEVADA also suffered varying degrees
of damage in the first half hour of the raid.

There was a short lull in the fury of the attack at about 8:30 a.m. At that time the USS NEVADA, despite her wounds, managed to get underway and move down the channel toward the open sea. Before she could clear the harbor, a second wave of 170 Japanese planes, launched 30 minutes after the first, appeared over the harbor. They concentrated their attacks on the moving battleship, hoping to sink her in the channel and block the narrow entrance to Pearl Harbor. On orders from the harbor control tower, the USS NEVADA beached herself at Hospital Point and the channel remained clear.

When the attack ended shortly before 10:00 a.m., less than two hours after it began, the American forces had paid a fearful price. Twenty-one ships of the U.S. Pacific Fleet were sunk or damaged. Aircraft losses were 188 destroyed and 159 damaged, the majority hit before they had a chance to take off. American dead numbered 2,403. That figure included 68 civilians, most of them killed by improperly fused anti-aircraft shells landing in Honolulu. There were 2,278 military and civilian wounded.

Japanese losses were comparatively light. Twenty-nine planes, less than 10 percent of the attacking force, failed to return to their carriers.

The Japanese success was overwhelming, but it was not complete. They failed to damage any American aircraft carriers, which by a stoke of luck, had been absent from the harbor. They neglected to damage the shoreside facilities at the Pearl Harbor Naval Base, which played an important role in the Allied victory in World War II. American technological skill raised and repaired all but three of the ships sunk or damaged at Pearl Harbor. A divided nation was united and translated into a whole hearted commitment to victory in World War II.

After the two-hour air raid on December 7, 1941, the United States counted *2,403* Americans dead and *2,278* wounded.

In the next chapter we meet one of the wounded who went on to become an Undersecretary of the Navy.

Let the survivors' stories begin.

Source: Department of Defense

2

From Pearl Harbor
to the Pentagon

All U.S. military personnel who endured the Harbor horror stood tall in the eyes of their fellow Americans. An officer who had only *one* leg to stand on after the attack went on to become an Undersecretary of the Navy.

Ensign Joe Taussig, less than a year out of the Naval Academy, was Officer of the Deck aboard the battleship NEVADA when the Japanese attack began. Two hours later, 21-year-old Taussig was alive, but suffering from a wound that would claim one of his legs. He was determined to carry on a proud family tradition. Both his father and his grandfather were Admirals in the U.S. Navy. The younger Taussig was among the NEVADA crew members who were awarded Navy Crosses, and President Nixon appointed Joe Assistant Secretary of the Navy, a post he held until 1993.

The USS NEVADA was the oldest battleship present at Pearl Harbor on December 7, 1941. She was commissioned in 1916, and had a proud heritage. So proud, in fact, that Taussig recalled that members of her 1941 crew were disciplined for "fighting ashore" when crews from other ships boasted that their battleships were better than the NEVADA. Hours after a Saturday night shore leave in Hawaii, the NEVADA crew set about proving their convictions.

The spirit of survival is captured in the following account by Ensign Taussig who identified himself in the narrative as Officer of the Deck (OOD).

It is not clear who saw the first attacking planes. The Boatswain's Mate of the Watch observed the bombs falling on Ford Island concurrently with the OOD's seeing a torpedo plane drop a torpedo and peel off, displaying the red circles under the wing. The General Alarm was sounded, and by the time the OOD climbed the two ladders to the AA gun deck, all of the guns were firing. A Chief Petty Officer had taken a sledge and knocked the locks off the ready boxes. He had also seen to it that the firing cut-outs which restricted the guns from firing above a 65 degree angle (for safety in peace) had been pulled.

The OOD was also an AA Director officer. By the time he climbed the additional ladders to the sky control platform, his director was already tracking a bomber. It was obvious that with so many AA bursts in the air, that no one had any idea which batteries from which ships were tracking the same aircraft. Mitsuo Fuchida, who led the air attack, noted in his writings how surprised he was that there was so much anti-aircraft fire so quickly.

In reality the duel between the AA guns and bombers was a standoff. The bombers were very inaccurate, and the AA fire was very inaccurate. The gun directors using analog gears would calculate the course, speed, height, and range to a bomber, and then calculate the fuse setting necessary to hit the enemy. The director then sent signals to each gun, activating pointers which instructed the crews to match the signals. Because of competitive judging practices, the guns were never fired at targets approaching more than 45 degrees ahead or aft of the beam, or flying less than 8,000 feet or more than 10,000 feet at a speed between 100 and 120 knots. Even with these "given" the accuracy of the guns was not good.

The bombers were even less accurate, as they had no way to calculate the winds, nor bomb sights capable of translating the height, course, or speed of the aircraft into a solution for accurate targeting.

The Japanese assigned four torpedo planes to attack the NEVADA. During survey operations in 1990, one of these torpedoes was found in the mud off the NEVADA moorings. Two torpedo planes were also found in the mud, one slightly forward of the beam and one slightly aft of the beam of the NEVADA's moorings. It is believed that one was shot down by the Marines in the "bird bath" and the other by a sailor on the mid-mast platform. Only one torpedo struck NEVADA, on the port side at about number 2 turret. This left a 35' X 40' hole in her side. Because the ship was well closed up, the flooding was confined to the proximate compartments.

The other battleships and the cruiser HELENA were not so fortunate. The three battleships nested outboard of the others all sank from torpedo hits, the OKLAHOMA rolling over.

In the initial dive bombing attacks, bombs exploded on NEVADA's forecastle and one amidships on the starboard side, starting fires in both instances. The dive bombers returned to strafe, and several men were killed or wounded, **including the Officer of the Deck** [reference to Taussig] **who was severely wounded by a bullet**

which passed completely through his thigh. *Dur-ing this phase of the attack, the USS ARIZONA blew up at the moorings directly ahead of the NEVADA, shower-ing NEVADA with a great deal of debris, and injuring or killing other personnel.*

A fleet signal was made for all ships to sortie. Because the NEVADA's boilers were not "cold" the ship was able to get underway in record time. By this time, the 19-year-old JOOD had also been wounded, and the conning of the ship was left to the ship's Chief Quartermaster. With ARIZONA burning furiously ahead, and a dredging line off the stern, the maneuvering of the ship was a master-piece of seamanship.

As NEVADA passed close by ARIZONA, additional fires broke out on our starboard side. Most were not se-vere, but burned several crewmen who refused to leave their AA guns. During the sortie, the second wave of attackers appeared, and chose NEVADA as the main target since she was by far the largest ship underway. There was ter-rible carnage on the AA deck. Out of the 90 officers and men assigned to the batteries, and the personnel who served as relief crews, fifty men were killed and over 100 wounded. Yet, throughout the battle, all guns were kept continuously in action. Only one AA officer escaped wounds; all of the CPOs were killed or wounded; and only three of the Gun Captains escaped death or wounds.

As NEVADA sortied, crews of other ships who saw her stopped for a moment and cheered. The bombs from the second attack left fourteen fires burning from hits and near misses, with a massive fire on the forecastle from a fire that ignited the ship's aviation gasoline and its paint locker. In order to save the forward magazines, more counter flooding forward was ordered, making the NE-VADA appear to be sinking by the head.

Fearing a third attack which might sink the ship in the channel, she was ordered to run aground near dry dock #1. This signal was ignored, and an emergency flag placed above it, and the ship reluctantly was grounded at Hospital Point.

More Congressional Medals of Honor and more Navy Crosses were awarded the crew members for their conduct during the Japanese attack than had ever been awarded to any ship's crew -- before or after. There were many hundreds of acts of bravery that went unnoticed on practically every ship present. **There is no record of a single person involved in the attack, whether in the Army, the Army Air Corps, Marine Corps or the Navy failing to do their best for their defense.**

Captain Joseph K. Taussig Jr. died in 2000, at the age of 81. His widow is writing a book about her husband's Navy career.

3

It Was No Prank

When an Army sergeant at Wheeler Field was awakened by aircraft noises unusual for a Sunday morning, his initial reaction was that "Navy flyboys" were playing a prank. But **Sgt. Leo Sienkiewicz** quickly discovered it was no joke.

Sixty years later, at his home in Pfafftown, North Carolina, Sienkiewicz had vivid memories of his wake-up call.

> *I was a staff sergeant with the U.S. Army Air Corps stationed at Wheeler Field, Hawaii, and assigned to the 73rd Pursuit Squadron, which had P40-E Curtis Warhawk pursuit airplanes. I was assigned as a crew chief to one of the airplanes.*
>
> *Since the United States was at peace our normal routine was each Saturday morning to hold personnel and aircraft inspection at the hangar area and after the inspection the personnel were excused from duty until Monday morning, other than those who had assigned duties for the weekend.*

December 7th morning I didn't get up early for break-
fast for I was going to sleep in. But at 7:50a.m. I was
awakened by sounds of diving airplanes. I figured it was
some Navy flyboys buzzing our barracks as a morning
prank. I turned over to go back to sleep but a few seconds
later the barracks was rocked by a loud explosion.

I jumped out of my bunk and ran to the window to see
an airplane flying so low that I could see the pilot and the
insignia on the side of the plane's fuselage. There was a
big red meatball on it. I said, "That's the damn Japanese;
what are they doing here?" I told my bunkie that some-
thing was wrong and that the Japanese are attacking
Wheeler Field. He said, "It can't be; that's just our Navy."

After leaving the barracks, a few hundred feet away
men were running around with blood coming down from
their faces and torn clothing. As I approached our hangar
I noticed a part of an arm hanging from a tree and
figured it was someone's arm blown off by the concussion
of a bomb that hit the barracks next to the hangar.

Arriving at the hangars we saw most of our airplanes
were damaged and burning. We started to salvage some
of the planes and had three planes in the air before the
second attack. Fortunately, the Japanese only strafed our
field and little damage was done. Our three fighter planes
downed three Japanese aircraft.

As the second wave flew by we noticed several B-17
bombers were flying in from the mainland and trying to
land at Wheeler Field. Our airmen opened fire on the
bombers, thinking they were Japanese aircraft. I saw B-
17s when I was stationed at Langley Field, Virginia, so I
ran around screaming that the airplanes were friendly
B-17s. Luckily, the bombers were not damaged by friendly
fire.

Several days after the attack I was informed that the hand I witnessed en route to the hangar was that of James M. Barksdale. He, with 10 other airmen including myself, brought more than forty P-40-E pursuit planes to Wheeler on the USS LEXINGTON in March, 1941.

During the attack on Pearl Harbor our unit lost 15 airmen and one pilot. Our squadron was sent to reinforce and protect Midway Island, and we remained on Midway for eight months.

After 44 months overseas I was discharged from the Army Air Corps. I later went to work for N.A.S.A., and retired in 1979 for health reasons. At present (2001) I am the North Carolina state chairman of the Pearl Harbor Survivors Association.

Aloha.

WWII photo of Howard G. Lee supplied by Mr. Lee.

4

Lives Saved by Enemy Oversight

Looking back over six decades, **Howard G. Lee** of Tennessee is still grateful for a big blunder made by the Japanese in their sneak attack on Pearl Harbor.

Petty Officer Second Class Lee was on board a loaded Navy fuel tanker docked between the battleships OKLAHOMA and CALIFORNIA the morning of December 7. Japanese "intelligence" apparently failed to detect the presence — or the importance — of the USS NEOSHO. Consequently, none of their firepower was directed at the sitting duck. Lee and his shipmates on the NEOSHO likely would have perished in a huge explosion if a Japanese torpedo had hit the volatile tanker.

Even without direct hits from Japanese planes, the ship that was given to the Navy by the Esso Oil Company remained in jeopardy. As the outgoing tide brought burning fuel on the water closer to the tanker, its skipper wisely moved the vulnerable vessel to a safer location on Ford Island. The Japanese pilots continued to ignore the moving target.

A December 8 entry in Howard Lee's diary describes the close call. "We are still trying to figure how the hell we got out of that inferno yesterday morning. We were sitting on a powder keg with burning oil all around us."

Former Eagle Scout Howard Lee joined the Navy in 1938 at the age of 20. At Pearl Harbor he was assigned to the USS ARGONNE, a supply ship. Trained as a photographer, he was a member of the Fleet Camera Party. Lee was granted a leave stateside, and was scheduled to return to California the afternoon of December 7 on the USS NEOSHO. He boarded the tanker Saturday evening, December 6, as a passenger. Sunday morning after breakfast he went topside and was waiting for "colors" (flag raising) on the stack deck at the stern of the ship.

Lee says he saw planes approaching, but he thought they were from the aircraft carrier USS ENTERPRISE, which was due in from sea maneuvers. Suddenly he saw a hangar roof on Ford Island "jump up in the air." When he looked back at the aircraft he saw the Japanese sun insignia. "We knew there were serious talks underway in Washington, but we never expected anything like this. We didn't lay a glove on them for the first two or three minutes." Lee said it looked like the torpedo planes were coming for the NEOSHO. As it turned out , the attackers were aiming for the ship in the next berth: the battleship OKLAHOMA.

Lee recalls, "If the Japanese had hit us first, it would have changed the picture of Pearl Harbor considerably." Instead, a mighty fighting ship became the first casualty of the day. "In the first ten minutes or less the OKLAHOMA just rolled over, upside down," according to Lee. "I was 100 yards away and watched the OKLAHOMA capsize." The scene was recorded in Lee's mind but not on film. The young Navy photographer's camera was locked up in the skipper's safe.

After the OKLAHOMA flipped, Lee says he saw at least one crew member surface from below in a large air bubble. Lee also witnessed others struggling in the water, but he said the Officer of the Deck would not allow anyone from the NEOSHO to leave ship to help them. Lee described something even more disturbing. "A lot of wounded and dazed men were seen being strafed by Jap planes after escaping from the OKLAHOMA. That's lower than anything I've ever seen or heard of."

The "passengers" on the NEOSHO felt helpless as they watched the carnage continue. "We witnessed hits on the USS WEST VIRGINIA and the USS ARIZONA. When the ARIZONA blew up it showered the Harbor with oil." Lee's diary notes that he saw the ARIZONA still burning 36 hours after the attack. While the NEOSHO was backing away from the dock, Lee watched the battleship NEVADA try to leave the Harbor. "We saw at least five direct hits by dive bombers on the NEVADA." He remembers seeing gun crews on the NEVADA's boat deck being knocked out.

Howard Lee related two unusual developments that are rarely discussed in connection with the events surrounding the attack on Pearl Harbor. After dark on the night of December 7, Lee says about five U.S. Navy dive bombers from the aircraft carrier ENTERPRISE tried to fly into Pearl Harbor. There were no lights on shore and only flames from burning ships illuminated the harbor. It is understandable why "everyone was trigger happy," as Lee puts it, and several of the Navy planes were shot down by friendly fire. By the light of day Lee saw the wreckage of one of the planes. "There was never an explanation given to my knowledge why the U.S. planes were sent to Pearl Harbor that night," Lee said.

Lee and other personnel on the NEOSHO spent the night of December 7 on the deck with rifles by their side. Sleep was hard to come by, and sometime after midnight Lee was awakened by unusual sounds. He looked up to see the giant aircraft carrier ENTERPRISE along side the tanker being refueled. After refueling, the ENTERPRISE disappeared into the night again. To this day Lee believes the fleet's aircraft carriers were on the Pearl City side of Hawaii during the attack.

In an interview for this book , Lee was asked about his state of mind immediately after the attack.

I wasn't scared. I was more mad and upset than anything else. We wanted every Japanese within a thousand miles to be dead. These clowns had stabbed us in the back with absolutely no warning. In fact this was against the way the Japanese really did things. They didn't believe in sneaking up on somebody and killing him. They believed in sneaking up on him, waking him up, and then killing him. Get his attention; let him know you are there, and then kill him. But they came right out of the clouds and nailed us good. If we had five minutes notice that they were coming we would have knocked their tails off.

I don't get emotional over losses at Pearl Harbor, but even today I get emotional when I hear the National Anthem. What impressed me more than anything else was the way the American public got into the act. They were all for one and one for all. The American people have never been so closely knit with one final objective in mind. I would like to see it right now like that.

After Pearl Harbor, Howard Lee continued a career of service to his country through the United States Navy. In

February, 1942, he was assigned to flight school at Pensacola Naval Air Base. Two weeks before he finished flight training, Lee married his Memphis sweetheart. After World War II, Lee returned to Pensacola as a flight instructor and retired from military service in 1960 as a Lieutenant Commander, USN.

Lee was a successful stock broker in Memphis until his retirement in 2001. At 83, he is in good health and stays active as a member of First Baptist Church in Memphis and president of a tri-state chapter of Pearl Harbor Survivors Association.

Lee enjoys speaking to high school and college students about his experiences. He usually closes his comments with this challenge:

> *Freedom is not free. Your freedom has been bought and paid for, and it is a gift to you. The payment is made by thousands upon thousands of people who are under all those crosses and markers in those national cemeteries. Be proud of the Flag. Be proud of the National Anthem. Be proud of the Pledge of Allegiance. Stand up and salute because you are an American, and your freedom has been paid for dearly by a lot of people.*

5

Leatherneck Luck

Today's youthful residents at Connie Maxwell Children's Home in South Carolina may dream about visiting the far-away island paradise of Hawaii.

But the trip for one alumnus of that faith-based facility turned into a hellish nightmare. On December 7, 1941, **Paul Morgan Adams** longed for the tranquility of the beautiful campus he left behind months earlier. Instead, Adams was aboard a battleship in Pearl Harbor targeted by Japanese bombs and torpedoes.

Coxswain Adams came close to being on the ill-fated USS ARIZONA, but by "the luck of the draw" he was assigned to the USS NEVADA. Here's how it happened, in survivor Adams' own words.

On June 21, 1941, I enlisted in the U.S. Marine Corps at Salt Lake City, although I was a South Carolina native. I was in the Civilian Conservation Corps (CCC) at the time of my enlistment. Upon completion of boot camp

*in San Diego, California, there were 36 Marines selected
from several recruit platoons for sea duty training. By September, 1941, we had completed the sea duty training.*

*It was at this time a battleship group consisting of
the USS ARIZONA, USS NEVADA and USS OKLA-
HOMA came into Long Beach with word that the ARI-
ZONA needed seven Marines. Our sergeant asked for seven
volunteers, and since all 36 men were anxious to leave the
recruit depot training environment at San Diego and go
to sea, all of us volunteered. He had us draw cards and
the men with the highest draw would report to the USS
ARIZONA. It was only a few days later that the remain-
ing 29 of my group, including me, were placed on the
Navy transport USS WHARTON for transfer to the Marine barracks at Pearl Harbor.*

*My wait for assignment to a ship's Marine detach-
ment was short. On October 4, 1941, I, along with four
other Marines, was transferred to the battleship USS
NEVADA, then at anchor in the harbor. Because I was a
new member in the Marine detachment, and the fact that
my last name started with the letter A, I was assigned to
mess duty for the month of December.*

*On Sunday morning, December 7, I was in the scul-
lery on the second deck washing the breakfast mess gear
when the general quarters was sounded. I thought it was
very strange that general quarters would be sounded on
Sunday morning with most of the officers and senior enlisted men ashore. The word was immediately passed over
the loud speaker, "Man your battle stations — we are under attack — this is no drill."*

*I grabbed my clothing and shoes and hastily ran to my
battle station at number seven 5-inch gun. While on the
way to my battle station, I felt the ship jump like it was*

out of the water and heard an explosion. It was a torpedo
that hit in the forward area of the ship on the port side at
about the location of the number one main battery turret.
*We immediately started getting bomb hits. One bomb hit
in the galley next to the number nine 5-inch gun, which
was adjacent to my gun, killing four Marines and seri-
ously wounding four other Marines. Another bomb hit the
bridge, killing three more Marines. Of the 76 Marines
on board the USS NEVADA, seven died during the attack
and 13 suffered wounds requiring hospitalization.*

*Very shortly word was passed that the battleship
OKLAHOMA was capsizing. Then I heard the loudest
explosion possible; it was the USS ARIZONA. Our ship
started to get underway while we were firing the 5-inch
broadside guns at the attacking planes with a slim chance
of downing one, but it kept us busy. As we got underway
and started down the main harbor channel, the Japanese
spotted us and concentrated their bombs on the NEVADA
in an attempt to sink us and block the channel. We took
five bomb hits in the forward area of the ship and were
told that we had at least 14 near misses, creating huge
geysers. Still underway, the NEVADA emerged from the
spray of bombs with her forward area and the main mast
on fire.*

*Fearing the ship would sink, we went aground, and
two yard tugs were sent to push the NEVADA from the
channel. We were pushed across the channel and beached
across from the southern end of Ford Island. After the
fires were brought under control, the dead and wounded
were removed from the ship. We learned that a large per-
centage of the ARIZONA crew had been killed and that
almost all of the Marine detachment had been killed, including seven Marines that I had trained with only five*

WWII photo of Paul M. Adams supplied by Mr. Adams.

months before. We also learned that a large number of men had been trapped in the USS OKLAHOMA when it capsized. Thirty-two men were rescued from the OKLA- HOMA, and I spoke with several of the men shortly after rescue at the Navy receiving barracks.

There were two Medals of Honor and 15 Navy Crosses awarded to the NEVADA'S officers and men for their gallantry during the Pearl Harbor attack. This was the largest number of medals ever awarded on any ship in the history of the Navy. Of the 29 Japanese planes shot down, two were credited to the USS NEVADA.

After nearly 60 years, the vivid memories of this ter- rible day still give me nightmares. The horrible realiza- tion was that I could have been aboard the USS ARI- ZONA, or a bomb could have hit my gun as well as the one next to mine.

At the time of his discharge from the Marine Corps in October, 1945, Paul Adams had decided that his future would be in California. He took advantage of the G.I. Bill educa- tion benefits by enrolling in Long Beach City College in 1946. After earning a degree in 1950, Adams became a civilian employee of the Navy in property management. In 1954, he accepted a property management position with the aviation company that was to become McDonnell-Douglas from which he retired in 1989.

In 2001, survivor Adams declared, "Due to some wise investments along with retirement pay and social security, my wife Gloria and I are able to enjoy a comfortable retire- ment in Cherry Valley, California."

The gregarious former Marine will never forget Pearl Harbor, but he also remembers his roots, according to Dr. Ben Davis, the Vice President of Connie Maxwell Children's

Home. "Paul Adams has always shown his gratitude for the care he received here by verbal affirmation, by staying in touch, by coming back 'home' for the reunion gatherings every other year, and through his financial support. In fact, Paul and his wife have established a trust that will benefit Connie Maxwell for years to come. We appreciate Paul for who he is, for his continuing love and support for this ministry and for his exemplary service to our nation during the Pearl Harbor battle and the ensuing war."

6

A Courageous Counterattack

Captain Charles H. Young concluded his military career as a meteorologist in the U.S. Air Force. But on December 7, 1941, the 19-year-old enlisted man wasn't concerned with weather conditions. It was the "rising sun" over Hickam Field that consumed his attention and nearly claimed his life.

The Pennsylvania native recalls how he and his Army Air Corps buddies launched a courageous counterattack against the Japanese.

I was assigned to the 42nd Bomb Squadron, 11th Bomb Group (H) at the time of the attack.

It was typical Sunday morning in the peacetime Army. Everyone was taking it easy. Ed Finn of Massachusetts and I knew that a flight of B-17s were due to arrive that morning. We were up and getting ready to leave and watch their arrival. We heard several explosions, and looked out the window on the Pearl Harbor side of the barracks and saw a low flying plane. As it banked around to the right, we could see the Japanese rising sun on the fuselage.

We were on the third floor of the barracks, and immediately rushed down the stairs and started across the road toward the ball field. The armament school was nearby, and Ed and I and a few others broke into the school. We obtained a .50 cal. machine gun and ammunition, then ran across the street to the ball diamond. Several machine guns, both .50 cal. and .30 cal. were obtained in this same way by others.

The aircraft that passed over the ball field came from the direction of the flight line and headed toward the harbor. The altitude of these aircraft was about 75 feet maximum. We were bombed, and as the planes banked around you could plainly see the pilot wearing goggles and helmet.

As I swung the .50 cal. toward the approaching aircraft, I could see smoke from the flight line, debris, and fire from the bombed hangars and aircraft that I knew were parked on the ramp. We saw B-17s that were part of the flight arriving from the mainland attempting to land. As I swung the .50 cal. around to follow the Japanese aircraft, I would end up facing the harbor. I could see the results of the tremendous explosions, thick black smoke, flames and Japanese planes diving over the harbor.

As far as damage to the Japanese aircraft, I remember we could follow the tracers into the passing planes. When I fired at one particular plane, I could see thick black smoke pour out of the cowling, then it banked out to sea and began a slow climb out. I do not know if the pilot went down or not. He could have made it back to carrier, or possibly have gone down at sea. Unless we could see the plane blow up as we were firing at it, we were not allowed to claim it as a shoot down.

At some time during the engagement, I was hit by something; maybe a bomb fragment, or possibly a piece of debris thrown up by a bomb blast. It wasn't anything serious, so I continued with what I was doing.

The lowest flying Japanese plane that I saw during the attack was a torpedo bomber that was not much higher than the barracks. It seemed as though every machine gun on the field was firing into it. The action took place over roughly a two-hour period, during which there was utter confusion.

After the attack was over, we were moved to another location near the base headquarters. Two days later we were relieved and returned to our own organization. Following my return to the mainland I was assigned to the CBI theater of operations. In 1942, Ed Finn and I were awarded the Silver Star and Purple Heart. I was discharged on June 5, 1945, a week short of five years of active duty.

Following WWII, Charles Young was recalled to the Air Force. After his military career, he was employed by Avco Space Systems, then retired to Jacksonville, where he serves as President of the Northeast Florida Chapter (6) of the Pearl Harbor Survivors Association.

Charles Young photo supplied by Mr. Young

7

A Nurse's Nightmare

Excerpt from Oral History of **Lieutenant Ruth Erickson**, *Nurse Corps, U.S.N.*
Lt. Erickson was a nurse at Naval Hospital Pearl Harbor during the attack.

We lived in temporary quarters directly across the street from the hospital, a one-story building in the shape of an E. The nursing staff had been increased to 30 and an appropriate number of doctors and corpsmen had been added. The Pacific Fleet had moved their base of operations from San Diego to Pearl Harbor. With this massive expansion, the hospital now operated at full capacity.

I had worked the afternoon duty on Saturday, December 6, from 3 p.m. until 10 p.m. with Sunday to be my day off. Two or three of us were sitting in the dining room Sunday morning having a late breakfast and talking over coffee. Suddenly we heard planes roaring overhead and we said, "The fly boys are really busy at Ford Island this morning." The island was directly across the channel from the hospital. We didn't think too much about it since the reserves were often there for weekend training. We no sooner got those words out when we started to hear noises that were foreign to us.

I leaped out of my chair and dashed to the nearest window in the corridor. Right then there was a plane flying directly over the top of our quarters, a one-story structure. The rising sun under the wing of the plane denoted the enemy. Had I known the pilot, one could almost see his features around his goggles. He was obviously saving his ammunition for the ships. Just down the row, all the ships were sitting there: the CALIFORNIA, ARIZONA, OKLAHOMA, and others.

My heart was racing, the telephone was ringing, the chief nurse, Gertrude Arnest, was saying, "Girls, get into your uniforms at once. This is the real thing!" I was in my room by that time changing into uniform. It was getting dusky, almost like evening. It was smoke rising from the burning ships.

I dashed across the street, through a shrapnel shower, got into the lanai and just stood still for a second, as were a couple of doctors. I felt like I was frozen to the ground, but it was only a split second. I ran to the orthopedic dressing room but it was locked. A corpsman ran to the Officer-of-the-Day desk for the keys. It seemed like an eternity before he returned and the room was opened. We drew water into every container we could find and set up the instrument boiler. Fortunately, we still had electricity and water. Dr. Brunson, the chief of medicine, was making sick call when the bombing started. When he was finished, he was to play golf — a phrase never to be uttered again.

The first patient came into our dressing room at 8:25 a.m. with a large opening in his abdomen and bleeding profusely. They started an intravenous and transfusion. I can still see the tremor of Dr. Brunson's hand as he picked up the needle. Everyone was terrified. The patient died within the hour.

Then the burned patients streamed in. The USS NEVADA had managed some steam and attempted to get out of the channel. They were unable to make it and went aground on Hospital Point right near the hospital. There was heavy oil on the water and the men dived off the ship and swam through these waters to Hospital Point, not too great a distance, but when one is burned — how they ever managed, I'll never know. The tropical dress at the time was white t-shirts and shorts. The burns began where the pants ended. Bared arms and faces were plentiful. Personnel retrieved a supply of flit guns from stock. We filled those with tannic acid to spray burned bodies. Then we gave these gravely injured patients sedatives for their intense pain. Orthopedic patients were eased out of their beds with no time for linen changes as an unending stream of burn patients continued until mid afternoon. A doctor, who several days before had renal surgery and was still convalescing, got out of his bed and began to assist the other doctors.

Do you recall the Japanese plane that was shot down and crashed into the tennis court?

Yes, the laboratory was next to the tennis court. The plane sheared off a corner of the laboratory and a number of the lab animals — rats and guinea pigs — were destroyed. Dr. Shaver, the chief pathologist, was very upset.

About noon the galley personnel came around with sandwiches and cold drinks; we ate on the run. About two o'clock the chief nurse was making rounds to check on all the units and arrange relief schedules. I was relieved around 4 p.m. and went over to the nurses quarters where everything was intact. I freshened up, had something to eat, and went back on duty at 8 p.m. I was scheduled to report to a surgical unit. By now it was dark and we worked with flashlights. The maintenance people and anyone else who could manage a hammer and nails were putting up black drapes or black paper to seal the crevices against any light that might stream to the outside.

About ten or eleven o'clock, there were planes overhead. I really hadn't felt frightened until this particular time. My knees were knocking together and the patients were calling, "Nurse, nurse!" The other nurse and I went to them, held their hands a few moments, and then went to others. The priest was a very busy man. The noise ended very quickly and the word got around that these were our own planes.

What do you remember when daylight came?

I worked until midnight on that ward and then was directed to go down to the basement level in the main hospital building. Here the dependents — the women and children — the families of the doctors and other staff officers were placed for the night. There were ample blankets and pillows. We lay body to body along the walls of the basement. The children were frightened and the adults tense. It was not a very restful night for anyone. Everyone was relieved to see daylight. At 6 a.m. I returned to the quarters, showered, had breakfast, and reported to a medical ward. There were more burn cases and I spent a week there.

On the evening of December 17, the chief nurse told me I was being ordered to temporary duty and I was to go to quarters, pack a bag, and be ready to leave at noon. When I asked where I was going, she said she had no idea. The commanding officer ordered her to obtain three nurses and they were to be in uniform. In that era we had no outdoor uniforms, thus it would be the regular white ward uniforms. We three nurses and a number of corpsmen from the hospital were assigned to the USS COOLIDGE. Eight volunteer nurses from the Queens Hospital in Honolulu were attached to the Army transport at the next pier (U.S.Army transport SCOTT, a smaller ship). The naval hospital brought our supplies the following day, the 18th, and we worked late into the evening. We received our patients from the hospital on the 19th— the COOLIDGE with 125 patients and the SCOTT with 55.

We left in the late afternoon of the 19th. There were eight or ten ships in the convoy. It was quite chilly the next day; I later learned that we had gone fairly far north instead of directly across. The rumors were rampant that a submarine was seen. I never get seasick and enjoy a bit of heavy seas, but this was different! Ventilation was limited by reason of sealed portholes and only added to gastric misery. I was squared about very soon.

The night before we got into port, we lost a patient, an older man, perhaps a chief. He had been badly burned. He was losing intravenous fluids faster than they could be replaced. Our destination became San Francisco with 124 patients and one deceased.

We arrived at 8 a.m. on Christmas Day! Two ferries were waiting there for us with cots aboard and ambulances from the naval hospital at Mare Island and nearby civilian hospitals. The Red Cross was a cheerful sight with donuts and coffee.

Our arrival was kept very quiet. Heretofore, all ships' movements were published in the daily paper but since the war had started, this had ceased. I don't recall that the other ships in the convoy came in with us except for the SCOTT. We were the only ships to enter the port. The convoy probably slipped away.

While at Mare Island, a doctor said to me, "For God's sake, Ruth, what happened out there? We don't know a thing." He had been on the ARIZONA, but was detached only a few months prior to the attack.

Editor's note: After WWII, Ruth Alice Erickson was promoted to the rank of Captain and appointed Director of the U.S. Navy Nurse Corps in Washington.

Captain Ruth Erickson
U.S. Navy Nurse Corps

Source: Department of the Navy, Naval Historical Center, Washington, DC 20374-5060

8

From Cook to Rescuer

Alonza Grant survived Pearl to return to Charleston, South Carolina, where he was born in 1919. Before he came home, Grant had served on six Navy ships.

On the morning of December 7, 1941, he was aboard the USS AVOCET, a seagoing tug that was moored at Ford Island in Pearl Harbor. Officer's Cook 2/c Grant was preparing a Sunday breakfast when he first heard the sound of unwelcome aircraft.

"The Japanese were strafing and bombing. So we immediately went into General Quarters to retaliate as best a small craft could. It really was a surprise attack. The Japs targeted all large ships and Army airbases.

"The AVOCET was not hit, but the dock caught fire and we had to move. We went around the harbor assisting ships and personnel in water that was covered with oil from the hit ships. Battleships and cruisers were burning which formed a black cloud over the harbor, seeming like night.

"When the second wave of planes attacked, the Japs tried to sink a battleship in the mouth of the harbor entrance/exit. It is very narrow there, and two ships could not pass. However the battleship crew beached the ship so not to block the harbor. When night came after that long day, there was a black-out. It was shoot and ask questions later.

"If the Japanese could see what damage they did, and if they had the manpower — they could have moved in and taken over the harbor. But the burning oil created a cloud that worked in our favor. It gave us time to clean up and recoup until the word got around and help came. The world found out about Pearl Harbor."

Indeed, and now the world needs to remember the veterans who died, or faced death, at Pearl Harbor in their duty

to the United States and the cause of freedom. Grant's military awards include the American Defense Ribbon, a Silver Star and three Bronze Stars. He is a widower whose daughter is a medical doctor.

A retired machinist foreman, Grant now volunteers as a Boy Scout leader, and he attends a Baptist church in Charleston.

WWII photo of Alonza Grant supplied by Mr. Grant.

9

Trapped Below?

On the deck of the battleship CALIFORNIA, the fight was against enemy planes. Below deck, **Ensign W.A.J. Lewis** was fighting flames. Lewis describes the scene:

General Quarters was sounded and I proceeded at once to the Forward Engine Room. The room was fully manned within a few minutes and I gave the order to set all condition on the Damage Control Fittings. We had just shifted Fuel Oil suction to the starboard battle tanker when we got the word from the oil king to make the shift. I checked the light and power machines and found them operating properly. I instructed the watch to watch all trips closely and if anything tripped out to reset it and hold it in if necessary.

The first torpedo hit came just as I was reaching the engine room. It knocked out about one half of the lights in the machine shop and about one fourth of the lights in the engine room. No machinery was tripped or put out of

*commission by this hit. An inspection of the engine room
showed that we had suffered no visible damage. I ordered
a main feed pump put on the line along with both main
fuel oil pumps. We had just started warming up the main
plant when we got reports that #1 boiler was getting water
in its fuel oil. Steam pressure dropped rapidly so we secured from warming up main set, secured main circulator,
and steam fuel oil pumps.*

*After the second torpedo hit, we began to get large
quantities of smoke down the ventilator blowers so we
secured the ventilators. Smoke still came down and word
was received that gas was present. We could detect nothing but powder gases so did not put on gas masks. Later
on the smoke became thicker so I directed some of the men
to put on their masks. They found a certain amount of
relief by doing so; mainly I think because it took certain
irritating particles out of the air and also because it pro-
tected the eyes. The smoke seemed to be coming now from
burning paint rather than powder. The smoke began to
take effect on the crew so I ordered all hands except the
talker on the upper level to go down to the lower level
where air was somewhat better.*

*The forward part of the engine room had become very
hot and the metal in some places was too hot to touch.
This accounted for some of the paint fumes as the paint
had begun to blister. When the order came to abandon
ship, (we did not receive the first order) I could not get the
watertight door above the hatch open. We then tried to
open the forward hatch but metal in that area was so hot
that it led us to believe that there was a big fire just above
us. We got all the fire extinguishers in the engine room
and all the extra clothes we could find to wrap around
ourselves and began to try to force the forward hatch. At*

about this time we were assisted from above and the hatch was opened. The fire was just forward of us so we proceeded aft and came up on deck. By this time the ship had been abandoned but the crew was rapidly returning to fight the fire in the midships Section.

The conduct of the crew was excellent. There was no confusion and each man manned his station and obeyed orders without question or delay; even at the time when all hands began to feel that we were going to be trapped below there was no hysteria or excitement.

USS CALIFORNIA (foreground) and USS NEOSHO (background) during the attack. Photo submitted by Howard Lee.

Source: Department of the Navy - Naval Historical Center Washington, DC

Bill Boggs on porch of his South Carolina home, displays medals *(photo by Dick Jensen)*.

10

Prayer Helped Gunner

Bright Sunday mornings are usually peaceful and calm for Fountain Inn, South Carolina, resident **Bill Boggs.** Most of the ones he's seen have been no different from any other — except for one special Sunday when he almost lost his life at Pearl Harbor.

"I was there when the Japanese attacked us that morning," Boggs said. "It's not a pleasant memory, but it's one I can't forget."

The road to Pearl Harbor was a lot shorter for William A. Boggs than the road back. When he enlisted in the Navy in January, 1938, he was only 21 and the threat of war was still far away in Europe. He was initially stationed at Norfolk, Virginia, but before the year was out he was commissioned to the USS HONOLULU in Brooklyn, New York.

"By 1941, it seemed war was imminent between us and Japan," Boggs said. So to protect our interests in the Pacific, Roosevelt sent us to Pearl Harbor on the Hawaiian island of Oahu."

Admiral Husband E. Kimmel was in charge of the fleet, and Lt. General Walter Short was in charge of the Hawaiian ground troops. Radar was set up to detect enemy aircraft, fighter planes were kept ready at nearby Wheeler field and troops drilled for action. Boggs, serving as a gunner's mate third class, was responsible for keeping anti-aircraft guns maintained and ready to fire. He usually slept in on Sundays, but that morning he was up early for shore patrol duty in Honolulu.

'I was up on the quarter deck in my dress blues and was getting ready to leave," he said. "The time was about 7:55 a.m., and everybody was expecting a nice, beautiful Sunday to take things easy."

Just then, he looked up to see a squadron of Japanese bombers flying overhead. In a few moments, they streamed down on the fleet in four waves. Fighter planes came in first and destroyed 170 planes ... and killed pilots scrambling from their barracks to get to them. Boggs and the other gunners ran to every available anti-aircraft gun and opened fire, but were no match for the enemy bombers.

"Soon the whole place was smoke — just completely covered in smoke — and I saw people killed right before my eyes and boys jumping into the oil-soaked water of the harbor."

Just then a 500-pound bomb exploded between the USS HONOLULU and the pier. The force lifted the ship up, burst the main battery and ammunition magazines, and began flooding the ship with water.

Boggs continued:

We were lucky because we were on the opposite side of the harbor — not even a block from the battleships — and nothing ever hit us directly, and none of us on that boat were killed or injured. The bombs fell all around us and other ships were being blown up or rolled — they just rolled over into the water which was only 35-40 feet deep. After the planes left, we immediately unloaded all the ammunition from the ship in case they returned. Then we used motor launches to pull kids out of the water and oil, and get them to sick bay and the hospital and assure them that everything was all right. Lunch that day was roast beef with ketchup, and nobody could eat.

The attack had ended, but 25-year-old Boggs' Navy duties were just beginning. After Pearl Harbor, he was reassigned to the USS HORNET. In the next four years, he and the other men on that ship shot down 668 Japanese planes as the United States slowly turned the tide of the war and closed in on the Japanese mainland. Not until Japan surrendered on August 15, 1945 — 44 months and eight days after Pearl Harbor — did Boggs have his next truly peaceful morning.

After the war, Boggs received eight medals and 11 campaign ribbons, including the Presidential Unit Commendation, his favorite, given to him by President Harry S. Truman. Boggs retired from the Navy in 1957; from civil service in 1974; and from South Carolina National Bank in 1981.

But it is his memory of Pearl Harbor that remains most with him. "During the attack I prayed," he said with tears. "That took me all the way through it."

His wife, Barbara, said he wasn't alone in his prayers. "My parents were listening to a football game on radio that day when the news interrupted to say that Pearl Harbor had been bombed," she said. "And my daddy bowed his head and we all sat together and prayed for this boy I ended up marrying."

Pearl Harbor has remained with Bill Boggs in another unfortunate way. Commanders Kimmel and Short, who were blamed for the attack, were court-martialed and reduced in rank. "My organization, the Pearl Harbor Survivors Association, has gone before Congress and tried to clear their names. They were the fall guys set up to take the blame in order to cover up what really happened that day."

A lot of bright Sunday mornings have passed for Boggs since December 7, 1941, but none have come close to matching what he saw that terrible day. "It's been with me ever since. I carry it with me every day."

Barbara and Bill Boggs in their Fountain Inn, South Carolina home *(photo by Dick Jensen).*

This chapter abridged from an article by L.C. Leach III, published 12-1-1999, in the TRIBUNE TIMES , Fountain Inn, SC.

Used with permission.

11

Rifle No Match
for Torpedoes

Like many young Marines, **Roy Capps** wouldn't make guard duty aboard ship his first choice of duty.

But ultimately, his name fell at the top of the list and the 18-year-old private first class couldn't refuse. So on December 4, 1941, he was transferred from a Pearl Harbor guard unit to duty aboard the nearby USS PENNSYLVANIA.

But on the night of December 6, he found Harold Comstock, a high-school classmate and fellow footballer, a sailor aboard the PENNSYLVANIA. The two went to a movie together that Saturday night.

The next morning, December 7, Capps stood his first guard duty aboard the 33,000-ton PENNSYLVANIA, which was in Dry Dock 1 for routine alignment of its propellers and shafts. He stood on the gangway when the first planes showed up.

"I couldn't believe what I saw, to begin with, because I knew we had no planes like that," Capps said. "And of course when they started dropping bombs, I was damned certain they weren't ours. Then you could see the rising sun on the aircraft and you knew who it was."

The crew was called to general quarters, but Capps was never relieved on the gangway. It turned out to be a lucky thing, because his battle station was on a 5-inch broadside gun.

"One of the bombs crashed through the boat deck and burst on the base of that gun, right where I would have been," he said. "So I got by that one easy enough."

Two sailors were manning a boiler alongside the ship while it was in dry dock. One of them got hit and Capps and the other sailor carried him to medical care on the quarterdeck.

"About that time the ship got hit again and we both went around and underneath this big pile of 12-by-12s they used to brace the ship up in dry dock," he said. They came out on the other side, in front of the destroyer SHAW, in floating dry dock more than a hundred yards away. The SHAW was hit by three bombs. "It blew up in our face, so we went back around the other way again," he said. "It was just all confusion. We couldn't do anything."

Harold Comstock, Capp's high school friend, was on a radio repair crew that was called to the quarterdeck. He was killed in a bomb blast.

Capps had a rifle and the usual five rounds of ammo given Marine guards, but he knew that was of no use against the planes.

"I could see the whole fleet get hit, practically," he said. "The only battleship I didn't see get hit was the UTAH, which was on the other side of Ford Island. The rest of them were torpedoed at anchor."

Fifteen members of the PENNSYLVANIA crew were killed and 38 were wounded. The PENNSYLVANIA was repaired and returned to service by December 20. For Capps, the Pearl Harbor attack was just the first action he saw in a 26-year Marine career. He was aboard the PENNSYLVA- NIA during fighting in the Aleutian Islands, then he joined the 5th and 6th Marine divisions and was with the latter for the bloody invasions of Okinawa in 1945.

Capps also served in the Vietnam War. He was awarded the Purple Heart when he was wounded during an attack by the Viet Cong, using captured U.S. mortars. He retired in March, 1968, as a master gunnery Sergeant at the Marine Corps Recruit Depot in San Diego, the same duty station where he began his career as a private 26 years earlier.

The Pearl Harbor attack, he remembers, was far differ- ent from anything else he experienced in his career. "The main thing was the surprise," he said. "Most of the other times we went into combat, we knew we were going into combat and we knew we were going to get action. But to just see everything being destroyed right in front of your eyes -- that was the biggest thing," he said. "It was a good thing the aircraft carriers weren't there; they'd gone to sea about three days before. That would have rally been hectic if they'd gotten those."

And as it turned out, the carriers' survival forced the U.S. to shift from reliance on battleships to aircraft carriers, the strategy many credit with winning the war in the Pa- cific.

Reprinted with permission from THE SUN newspaper in Bremerton, Wash- ington.

Frank Plyler flies Stars & Stripes with a PHSA banner at his North Carolina home in 2001 *(photo by Dick Jensen).*

Alice and Frank Plyler 60 years after Pearl Harbor *(photo by Dick Jensen).*

12

Real Romance Survives

In the summer of 2001, **Frank Plyler** watched a love story unfold during the movie "Pearl Harbor," and thought of his own. Miles away, on the other side of the city dark with heavy rain, Alice sat at home, waiting for him to return; Alice, his wife of 58 years, the woman who waited seven long days in 1941 to find out whether Frank had lived or died.

About the hardest part of surviving Pearl Harbor was being unable to tell your fiancee that you were OK. A world at war didn't care much about the future of two college sweethearts in love with the idea of spending a life together. The uncertainty Alice knew during those seven days and Frank's anxiety over her worry ... "was more tolerable then than it would be now," he said in his theater seat before the movie rolled. "We were both youngsters those 60-plus years ago. She sort of grows on you."

Frank and Alice have their own Pearl Harbor love story to tell. It begins like this:

The one thing young Frank didn't have was money. The middle in a family of three boys, he had loving parents and, because his father was a Methodist minister, a new home every few years. "We didn't have a little money, we had no money," he said in the home he shares with Alice.

One thing he did have, however, was a desire to go to college. Pfeiffer was a two-year college near his home in North Carolina. Newly graduated from high school, Frank and his mother went to see the president of the school to find out if there was any scholarship money for the following Fall. Might be, the president said. Would you be willing to work on the school farm? Are you kidding, Plyler thought.

The next Monday, he moved into the bunkhouse on the farm with three other students. They worked that summer to supply the milk and vegetables needed by people attending conferences at the Methodist school. Every so often, it was his turn to push the cart of milk and cream to the dining hall. That was the first time Alice Bennett, attending one of the conferences, saw him. Bennett, the youngest of three children of a farming family who lived near Franklin, North Carolina, wasn't impressed. They were both freshmen. He saw her around and she saw him, but neither showed interest in the other.

Then one day he was in the parlor of a dormitory, on a date with another girl, when Alice sneaked up on them to aggravate the girl, a friend of hers. She gave Frank a piece of candy. "I said, 'I need to know that girl.' There was something about her. She wasn't raunchy and loud, but there was something about her attitude that attracted me. I said, 'She's the one for me.'"

Their first date was on Valentine's Day, 1938, at a party the college threw. "We just clicked," Alice recalled. "We started talking. We're alike as two peas in a pod. We have the same ambitions, we have the same values. I think we read each other's minds."

They were together throughout their two years at Pfeiffer, and they were informally engaged by the time they started at Western Carolina Teachers College in 1939. But with the transfer came the end of Frank's job at Pfeiffer, and after a semester at the school in Cullowhee, North Carolina, he was out of money. Germany had invaded Poland, and Britain and France had declared war on Germany. Japanese forces were pushing into China and had their eyes on creating an empire in southeast Asia.

Plyler, out of money and out of options, decided to enlist in the Army during Christmas, 1939. The recruiter he signed up with refused to send him to the Philippines — Plyler's request — because Frank had no military experience. If Japan were to strike U.S. forces anywhere, it would be there, the recruiter said. Instead, he sent Plyler to an Army vacancy in Hawaii.

Alice, at home for the holidays with her family, didn't know what Frank had done. "I probably would have tried to talk him out of it," she said. "But I really had no real problem with it. I was young and foolish in those days, but we weren't foolish enough to get married. We each had our own job to do. Neither one of us had anything to start a marriage on. We were both level-headed people. We knew the responsibilities and all that goes with marriage."

Still, Frank responds, "it was like cutting off an arm" to leave her. He shipped out to Hawaii, and she went to teach in a small one-room schoolhouse in Nantahala, about half an hour's drive from her parent's home. There were no phones and no electricity in the community. All Alice had that connected her to Frank were the twice-weekly letters she would send and receive, and the knowledge — the hope — that she would see him again one day.

Plyler was assigned to the 25th Infantry division and quartered at Schofield Barracks on the Hawaiian island of Oahu. The eight battleships of the U.S. Pacific Fleet were moored in Pearl Harbor, one of the world's largest and best-sheltered naval anchorages, on the south side of the island. Plyler's first job was to drive an ambulance. Then he moved up to the motor pool to be placed in charge of a 100-man unit maintaining and driving some four dozen vehicles. After nearly two years on the island — two years of not seeing Alice — he was a master sergeant. Twenty-one years old, he was writing her twice a week. She was writing him about the same.

On December 6, 1941, Plyler was in the field, checking his vehicles and the men detailed to other Army divisions protecting the south side of Oahu. The soldiers had been on red alert, the highest possible, for weeks and were relieved when it was reduced to no alert that day. It meant they could leave the field and go back to the barracks.

"That has always been a puzzler to me — why the alert was called off," Plyler wonders. "We knew they were going to hit us. But we thought it would be the Philippines." He was so happy about the prospect of a good night's sleep in a decent bunk, however, to think much about it at the time. December 7 was a Sunday, which meant sleeping in, at least until the 8 a.m. air show the Army Air Corps would stage at Wheeler Field.

Sunday morning he was miffed. At 7:50 a.m., he heard engines coming over the mountains that ringed Schofield Barracks. He ran outside to see if the planes had started early. They did, all right. They were coming for him — dozens of them, spaced evenly throughout the sky. All the planes veered toward the harbor, except one. Suddenly the ground skittered toward him in little explosions. He didn't even think. He hit the ground spread-eagle, as he'd been taught, to dissipate any shock waves that would pulsate from a bomb. The aircraft perforated the barracks.

"I can still hear that," he said. The shell casings were hitting the ground louder than gunfire." It was about then he saw the "meatball," the Japanese insignia, on the wings. The ground was spraying all around him. "You don't feel you're breathing," he said, recounting the fear. "You don't feel the ground can give you any protection, but you're trying to get closer and closer to the ground."

The plane flew off, presumably to join the others strafing the harbor. Soldiers were pouring out of the barracks and into the transport trucks Plyler and his crews were loading. About half an hour later, they were back in their field positions, listening to the explosions in Wheeler Field, which the Japanese were also bombing

"We weren't in a position to do anything about it. That's a pretty helpless feeling," he said. "It was about as surprising an attack as could have been pulled off. I wouldn't have given you 30 cents for our chances to hold the island. We were wiped out," Plyler lamented.

At noon on December 7, Alice was sitting in the living room of the boarding house where she rented a room. She and the other boarders were listening to the owners sing gospel tunes when a bulletin broke though the radio program they had tuned in: Pearl harbor had been attacked.

Frank, she thought.

Despite the mounting tensions in the Pacific, she always had a feeling that Frank would be all right. "Call it faith, inner strength," she explained. Though she knew this meant war and though she had grown up during the Depression, she had no experience to tell her to be afraid for her fiancee. Instead, she had a deep, abiding knowledge, she claimed, that Frank would be OK.

But for days, there was no word of whether she was right. "Can you imagine, when you love someone and that you intend to spend your life with them, how you feel? You're naturally uneasy," she confessed.

Alice kept herself busy teaching her 30 students. Plyler, like other soldiers or sailors after the attack, was busy, too. While the Navy retrieved bodies and fixed what it could, the Army was reinforcing its position in the hills around the island in case of a follow-up attack. Plyler was worried for Alice, but he couldn't get away to send her a message.

Finally, a few days later, he was able to get to Wahiawa, a sugar cane village near Schofield Barracks, to send a telegram. "There was no way she would know how any of us turned out. I wished that she knew," he said.

Seven long days after the attack, Alice's brother came driving up to the boarding house with a telegram. Alice tore it open and poured over the message. "I remember those words. I know the words exactly."

Now decades later, she still listens for the sound of Frank's car pulling into the driveway. If he is gone longer than she thinks he should be, she gets worried. "He has some health problems, and that bothers me," Alice confides. "Actually, I think we both depend on each other. It takes both of us to keep going. In the whole world, he's the most important person, and I think I'm pretty important to him."

By Paul Clark, Copyright 2001, ASHEVILLE CITIZEN-TIMES. Reprinted with permission.

13

Six Decks Below

It wasn't until 24 hours later that **Bob Brown** realized how close he might have come to being a Pearl Harbor casualty.

The 19-year-old seaman first class was far below decks of the battleship USS MARYLAND, surrounded by 16-inch turret ammunition, when word came over the loudspeaker that the harbor was under attack.

That was all Brown and the seven or eight other men in the ship's magazine knew of the Japanese bombing. They couldn't hear a thing.

"It's hard to conceive that anything that makes as much noise as bombs falling couldn't be heard" he said, "but we were surrounded by tons and tons of armor and steel. We were six decks below where the action was taking place."

A safe place to be, it seems, until you consider what happened to men in similar positions aboard other Navy vessels.

The MARYLAND, tied up to a Ford Island mooring, lay inboard of the more exposed OKLAHOMA, which was struck by five torpedoes and turned over.

Several hundred yards away, the USS ARIZONA, also tied up alongside Ford Island, was hit by eight heavy bombs, detonating the ship's magazines and sinking it.

Brown and his shipmates knew nothing of this. They were at their battle stations but there was nothing they could do. The ammunition they were responsible for was to be used with 16-inch guns designed for bombardment of shore or other ships, not fighting enemy aircraft.

"It was a very helpless feeling," he said. "I wasn't scared. I don't know anyone down there who was. We just didn't know enough to be terrified."

After the attack, it was nightfall before Brown was able to climb topside.

"All we could see were the fires burning around the harbor — there was no other light," he said. "We were completely blacked out."

The next morning, after he was released from duty, he and some shipmates surveyed the damage. It wasn't until then that he realized how lucky he was. People in the same positions on other ships were killed.

The MARYLAND was hit by one bomb that struck the canvas awning across the forward end of the ship. Three sailors drowned when they became trapped in flooded compartments. The ship was repaired and was back at sea in early 1942.

For the rest of the war, Brown served on ammunition and cargo ships, and finally a new aircraft carrier. On the latter, his battle duty was as gunners mate in charge of antiaircraft battery at the edge of the flight deck, prime target for Kamikaze attacks.

But those attacks never came. Brown didn't know it at the time, but the carrier was headed to Japan for the planned invasion. The invasion never happened; the United States dropped two atomic bombs.

"The atom bomb saved my life and the lives of many, many more," Brown said.

Reprinted with permission from THE SUN newspaper in Bremerton, Washington.

14

Students Hear Survivors

"Veteran of attack by Japanese to speak at Greer school," was the newspaper headline announcing something **Hal C. Norman** is proud to do.

Norman, like many other Pearl Harbor survivors, eagerly accepts invitations to speak to student groups about the importance of understanding why December 7, 1941, was described as a "date that will live in infamy." And, like many Pearl survivors who talk on the subject, duty and sacrifice were Norman's themes to a fourth grade class on December 7, 2000.

Navy radioman Norman saw those same themes played out on a movie screen in Honolulu the night of December 6, 1941. He was watching "A Yank in the R.A.F." — a war film starring Tyrone Power and Betty Grable. As he left the theater that night, the young sailor had no idea that in less than 12 hours he would be in the vortex of one of history's most notorious military conflicts.

Norman was assigned to the USS ST. LOUIS, a light cruiser that escaped Pearl Harbor with only superficial damage. The ship normally carried four light-weight seaplanes —deployed as scouting aircraft—but the planes were shore-based at Ford Island for routine overhaul the weekend of the Japanese attack. Norman had maintenance duty in connection with the aircraft on Ford Island.

"I was sitting in the barracks talking to someone, just an early morning conversation," Norman recalls. "At the first explosion I heard, I thought one of our planes had crashed. Someone came through the barracks shouting, 'It's the real thing, it's the real thing.'"

Norman dashed toward one of the ST. LOUIS' seaplanes at the edge of the water. At about the same time a huge explosion rocked the nearby USS SHAW, showering debris over the entire area. Norman's main job then was to help move the vulnerable aircraft to cover. And what was going through the mind of this 21-year-old under fire? "Anger, more than anything else. Sometimes in situations like that, you don't have time to be afraid." That sentiment is a common refrain among Pearl survivors. Norman says he was changed by a "day you just can't forget."

In his eighth decade, the retired electronics salesman still does what he can to help students understand that day.

Hal Norman and his wife are residents of Taylors, South Carolina.

This chapter based on a report published in THE GREENVILLE NEWS (South Carolina)

15

Floridians Remember

Florida draws retirees like a magnet. Many members of the Pearl Harbor Survivors Association now reside in the Sunshine State. In an earlier chapter we met **Charles Young** of Jacksonville.

Another Floridian is a past-president of PHSA: **Ben C. Begley** of St. Petersburg. On December 7, 1941, he was the duty gunner aboard the USS DOBIN. Begley claims his ship fired the first shots at the attacking aircraft, downing one Japanese plane in the early moments of the encounter.

Another Pearl survivor who adopted Florida is **Billy J. Zachary.** From his home near St. Augustine, Zachary recalls his gruesome task aboard one of the hardest hit battleships:

I joined the United States Navy July 9, 1940, as an apprentice seaman. Upon completion of boot camp (in Norfolk, VA) I was transferred to the USS CALIFOR-NIA in Long Beach, CA, in October 1940. After about 4 or 5 weeks aboard the CALIFORNIA, I was transferred to the Flag allowance of Commander Battle Force Pacific Fleet commanded by Vice-Admiral Pye.

On December 6, 1941, I departed the ship for weekend liberty. I visited a friend from my home town in North Carolina who was stationed at Fort Kamehameha. We had an early breakfast and were going back to the barracks to change clothes when the raid began.

At first we thought the bombs were coast artillery guns and commented that we didn't know they were scheduled to practice today. About this time Jap fighters began strafing the base. We could also see the fighters and bombers over Hickam Field. I joined an Army Doctor and we proceeded to pick up wounded until I was able to get a ride back to Pearl Harbor Naval Station.

I was shocked at the sight of the Harbor. The USS CALIFORNIA was sinking, the OKLAHOMA had capsized and the ARIZONA was still burning. Upon boarding the CALIFORNIA, I was assigned to take a mattress bag and pick up body parts of men.

To keep the CALIFORNIA from capsizing, steel cables were wrapped around the turrets and cement key we were tied up to. Later in the day Admiral Pye transferred his command to the beach. The enlisted men were berthed at barracks at the submarine Base. I would like to add that the friend I was visiting (Paul Nanney) and I did not see each other again until December 7, 1998 (57 years later).

16

Ambulance Driver's Testimony

South Carolina newspaper reporter Mary Lane had never interviewed a veteran of the Pearl Harbor attack, and she knew time was not on her side. Only 92 Pearl Harbor survivors were still alive in her state 60 years after the historic battle. She learned that one of them lived in the same town where she worked, and he was chairman of the state chapter of the Pearl Harbor Survivors Association.

When Mary Lane called **Donald L. Ralph,** he was ready to talk.

Ralph was the oldest of nine children in a rural Kentucky family. "My people were farmers, and my dad worked in the oil fields. They struck oil in 1929, right before the depression, but my family were basically big farmers," Ralph said. "We raised tobacco, and I hated tobacco. That is one reason I joined the Army because I didn't want to work in it." Ralph said another reason that influenced him to enlist in the Army was the lack of excitement for a young man where he lived. "The Army paid $21 a month, which was more than I would make if I stayed at home and worked," Ralph reflected.

Don Ralph was sworn in the Army on July 4, 1940, at Fort Knox, Kentucky. When he signed up, the Army didn't have basic training because the draft had not started yet. Before he was shipped to his assignment, the young recruit went through a two week basic training. He was given a choice between serving in Hawaii or the Philippines. In October he arrived at Hickam Field, the Army Air Corps base adjacent to Pearl Harbor. Looking back, Ralph believes his choice was providential. "By the good Lord's grace I took the Hawaii assignment, otherwise I would have been in the Bataan death march when the Japanese hit in 1941."

Ralph worked as an x-ray technician in a new hospital at Pearl Harbor — soon to be tested to the max. Here's how he remembers December 7:

It was Sunday morning and pretty quiet. We did our job and that was it. It was not unusual for the Navy to do practice bombing, so when the first bomb hit, nobody thought anything about it until a few moments later when they realized it wasn't a practice routine; it was the real thing.

We had a first sergeant named Donald Rhodes who appeared in the hall and blew his whistle like they always do when they call everyone in assembly. Sgt. Rhodes said, "If I'm not mistaken, we've got a war going on. Get your full field packs on, get your canteens full of water and fall out in front. We'll be assigned to teams. You're going to find people with their arms off, their legs off, and their heads off. If their heads are off, don't bother them."

I was assigned to drive an ambulance, and we picked people up off the flight line and various places over the base and drove them to the hospital. Then we did first-aid

*type things because there were so many people. We took
some of them to Trippler General Hospital which was
only six miles away.*

Don Ralph returned to the mainland in April, 1943, and
remained in the Air Force until his military retirement in
1960. As a civilian, he went into the automobile business in
Massachusetts, before moving to South Carolina in 1963.

Ralph is not a movie critic, but he liked the 2001 film,
"Pearl Harbor." He and other Pearl survivors were given
free tickets to attend a showing at a Columbia theater. Here's
Ralph's take on the Hollywood version of what he witnessed
first hand six decades earlier:

*"It's a good movie. Some people complained that it
didn't show enough of this or that, but I enjoyed it. It was
very well done. It showed the human side of the war where
families were uprooted. I could relate to that because my
little grade school sweetheart was put by the wayside, and
I met another lady and married her."*

Don and Mary Elizabeth Ralph had been married 58
years when he was interviewed for this book.

The former ambulance driver for Uncle Sam discovered
the driving force for his life long ago. "I found Jesus and
became a Christian when I was 14 years old. I am still a
Christian, and I ask people if they're not, they should consider it."

---

*This chapter based on an exclusive interview conducted by Mary Evans Lane
of THE MANNING TIMES.*

17

A Cabby's Call to Arms

Sergeant Bill Crawford was awakened from his Sunday morning sleep by an urgent knock on the door of his Waikiki Beach cabin. When he opened the door, there stood a taxi driver. Crawford had neither called for a cab, nor was he prepared for what the cabby announced.

"The driver told me to report to my Army base because there was a war going on. I said, 'Man, don't give me that.' But he told me to turn on the radio in my room. He explained that my brother had called him and gave him my apartment number. So I turned on the radio. Sure enough they were telling everyone to stay inside and not use the telephones. I paid the cab driver, put on my clothes, and rushed to my base."

Sgt. William F. Crawford and his brother were both stationed at Fort DeRussy near Diamond Head. Bill Crawford was an information officer assigned to the HSCAV unit on the artillery base commanded by a General Burgin. Crawford had enlisted in the Army in 1936. Ft. DeRussy was about 15 miles south of Pearl Harbor and 30 miles from Wheeler Field. Therefore, Sgt. Crawford was not an eyewitness to the attack in progress, but he got an eyeful the next day.

"On Monday, Colonel Martin and I drove to Pearl Harbor, Hickam Field, Wheeler Field and Kaneohe Station to prepare a report for Gen. Burgin. We saw all the ships still burning in the harbor. At Hickam we saw our planes on the ground, and we saw hangars full of planes that had been bombed. It was evident to us that the Japanese knew which hangars to bomb. Hangars that were empty were not harmed. Same story at Wheeler Field. The spies had given last minute details of everything they needed so they didn't waste any bombs on empty hangars."

Another Pearl survivor affirmed Crawford's observation about the effectiveness of Japan's pre-invasion intelligence activity. Jack E. Williams, a Marine aboard the USS CALIFORNIA, wrote in 1998: "It was reported the Japanese had 157 espionage agents and 1,500 workers in the area. This is how they could name every ship and its location in the harbor." A sailor aboard a submarine tender added, "I saw the chart all Japanese pilots had strapped to leg clipboards showing the location of all ships in the harbor."

Crawford's inspection tour of Oahu Island turned up evidence of another piece of Japan's military strategy. "We saw a small submarine just off shore in Kaneohe Bay. It had run aground, and Col. Martin took this report back to Gen. Burgin, also."

Crawford remembers that there were anti-aircraft batteries scattered all over Oahu. But on that sleepy Sunday morning "hardly any of them had live ammunition," he declared. In spite of this handicap, Crawford claims "they did manage to knock down a couple of Japanese planes."

After his discharge in 1945, Bill Crawford operated a cab company in Honolulu before moving to South Carolina in 1949. The Army veteran managed the AMVETS Club in Greenville until 1986. Since then Crawford and his wife, Margaret, have enjoyed traveling and participating in the senior activities of White Oak Baptist Church in Greenville.

WWII photo of Bill Crawford supplied by Mr. Crawford.

18

"I Love You, Goodbye"

In hindsight, it was a sign of things to come.

Ken Freeberg, an 18-year old sailor aboard the light cruiser USS HONOLULU, remembers being on maneuvers in the Pacific the week before the Japanese turned warplanes upon Pearl Harbor. The ship went to battle stations, apparently because of fears it was being watched by a Japanese submarine.

Though the possible contact was reported, no one imagined a sneak attack was coming on December 7. "It was the furthest thing from our mind," Freeberg said. "The night before, everybody was in Honolulu raising hell."

The morning of the attack, Freeberg, who was a striker, or trainee, electrician at the time, was scrubbing the bunkroom deck when the call came for battle stations. He ran up to the main deck and looked over the stern to see a Japanese torpedo plane headed straight for the ship, tied up at the Navy yard. "And the damn thing blew up right in front of my eyes," Freeberg said.

He kept a diary of his experiences, and following are some excerpts of his descriptions of the Pearl Harbor bombing:

"0805: Torpedo planes were coming in just back of us, with shining torpedoes hanging and the rising sun on the side, and at the same time machine-gunning motor launches and everything else. They sure as hell had caught us with our pants down.

"The heat from our guns and the noise was terrific.... One poor kid on gun No.3 was so scared he ran in the O.D. booth on the quarterdeck and they had to drag him out....

"Over the loudspeakers came the word to get ready to get under way. I helped a first class boatswain tear the forward brow off and we tore the gangway lights off. We were throwing all unnecessary equipment out on the dock. All during this the bombers have been flying over us dropping bombs all over the harbor....We back away from the dock and then for some reason we moved up to the dock again."

Freeberg's battle station was on the quarterdeck; if bomb damage caused a power outage, it was his job to try to restore it. "We wandered around the deck while it was going on," he said. "If we got hit, then there would be something to do. And being a striker, I didn't know what the hell I would do."

More from the diary:

"0930: Dive bombers came in on us. There was still no sign of our planes. God, how they came down! The sky is covered with puffs of smoke from the anti-aircraft batteries....I went to the port side and was watching the dive bombers at the same time calling for the gunners to get those rats.

One bomb crashed into the pier next to the HONOLULU, smashing a hole in the ship's hull. The part of the ship where Freeberg had been mopping earlier that morning began to flood with water and oil, though the ship was never in danger of sinking. The HONOLULU escaped further damage and no crew members were injured. Freeberg and his shipmates remained at their battle stations the rest of the day.

More excerpts from his diary:

"1600: Survivors from the sunken ships start coming aboard. They tell us stories of how their ships got sunk and how they got away. The fire on the WEST VIRGINIA has been put out. She looks pretty bad but I think she will come through to fight again under better conditions. I hope.

"The ARIZONA is still burning, covering the sky with smoke. Everything looks eerie and silent. All the ship's guns are manned and ready for anything that might come...."

Air raid alarms sounded during that first night, but they were American planes.

Freeberg served aboard the HONOLULU and then the USS MONTPELIER throughout the war in the Pacific, ships that combined earned 21 stars. He was aboard for bombardments at the Aleutian Islands, Guadalcanal, Saipan, Guam and the battle of the Philippine Sea.

Through it all he kept the diary, which he now shares with his family, though he acknowledges he wasn't supposed to keep one. He kept it hidden under floorboards on the ships.

"That's what got me about being in the Navy," he said. "You weren't supposed to write anything down about where you were or what you were doing. What the hell could you write: 'I love you, goodbye?' "

"Who knows, I might have been court-martialed if they found out about it," he said. "I don't think they can do it now. Who the hell would have thought that 60 years later I'd be sitting here telling someone about all this?"

Reprinted with permission from THE SUN newspaper in Bremerton, Washington.

19

"The War's Started!"

FRANK MATTAUSCH and the other soldiers at Wheeler Field knew something was up. The Army base was placed on alert more than a week before December 7.

The Army Air Corps' 135 fighter planes, the main air defense for the island of Oahu, were sheltered around the edge of the air field inside more than 100 revetments, U-shaped earthen walls eight feet high that served as bunkers.

But on Friday, December 5, orders from the top came to remove the aircraft from those bunkers, and they were parked in front of the hangars. On Saturday, the pursuit squadrons decided to do some marching on the flight line and moved the aircraft together.

So when Mattausch, a machinist at the base, awoke at 7:30 on Sunday morning, December 7, the planes were out in the open along the hangars — in clear view and a perfect target. And despite the earlier alert, no one expected anything to happen. "We didn't think the Japanese would dare," Mattausch said.

Mattausch pulled on his trousers, socks and shoes and walked into the washroom. He was living in a barracks room with seven other sergeants, several of whom were still asleep. It was a little after 7:45 a.m. when he walked back into the room.

"Out the window we could see some planes that came through Kolekole Pass and headed past the mountains toward Pearl Harbor," Matausch said. "And just a second later another plane pulled out of a dive about 200 feet up, and a little black speck left the airplane." It might have been the first bomb of the Japanese attach on Hawaii and it hit Wheeler Field.

"As the bomb was still falling I remember somebody shook one of the guys who was sleeping and said, 'Wake up, Longdyke! The war's started!'" Mattausch recalled.

Mattausch grabbed the shirt and tie off his bed and ran down the hallway and down the stairs, getting dressed as he moved. And just then the Japanese bombed the hangar across the street from the barracks, about 50 feet away. The barracks shook violently but it wasn't hit.

He and six other men raced to a supply room they knew contained a .50-caliber machine gun on a tripod. It was locked up behind a wood-and chicken-wire partition, which they quickly yanked down.

They set the machine gun up on the back porch and Tech. Sgt. Bill Bayham, Mattausch's boss and a World War I veteran, began firing, shooting down one of the planes, according to the sergeant. Mattausch and six other men were given Army commendations for establishing machine gun firing positions in the midst of the bomb attack.

And days later, a Movietone newsreel crew shot some footage of Bill Bayham. "Bill's sister wrote that she was at a theater in Dayton, Ohio, and all of a sudden there's his picture on the screen," Mattausch said. "She yelled, "That's my brother!" Everybody clapped and they stopped it and ran it back through a few times."

Though the one hangar was the only one bombed, the damage to Wheeler was devastating. The base had no anti-aircraft guns or air raid shelters.

"The attack didn't last very long, and afterwards I went down on the flight line — just a whole bunch of burning planes." Thirty-four people were killed, mostly soldiers living in a tent city who were hit by stray Japanese machine gun fire during the attack. Ninety of the 135 planes were destroyed. Only 45 could be salvaged.

But one squadron from Wheeler had airplanes at a gunnery field on the north end of Oahu. Eight pilots drove to the gunnery field after the attack started and got their planes in the skies and shot down 12 enemy aircraft.

"That indicates how different the battle would have been if we'd been able to get all our planes into the air," Mattausch declared.

After the bombing, the Army feared the Japanese would be sending in paratroops, so the soldiers stayed up for three days guarding the air field, according to Mattausch. No one was allowed back in barracks. "We were just dead exhausted after that three days," he said.

Mattausch remained at Wheeler until 1942. Later he joined an outfit that traveled to the Gilbert Islands and set up an airfield on Makin after the Army infantry landing in 1943. His unit was in charge of aircraft maintenance and remained on the island for 11 months.

He asked to be able to go along on one flight for repair work to a B-25 bomber. He was granted permission and prepared to go, but for reasons he never learned, they left without him. The plane attempted to return after dark and the six-man crew, which included his commanding officer, was never found.

After the war, when Mattausch was working in Illinois, he read a newspaper article about the Japanese commander of Mili Island, 75 miles north of Makin, being tried for war crimes for beheading six Americans whose plane had mistakenly landed on Mili after becoming lost.

Reprinted with permission from THE SUN newspaper in Bremerton, Washington.

20

Beyond Survival

A Tribute to Pearl Harbor Survivors
by Dick Jensen

What can I write about Pearl Harbor survivors that hasn't already been written or spoken?

What if I called you "survivalists"rather than survivors?

The English word "survivor" has been around for about 400 years. But "survivalist" is a relatively new word. It was not in 1941 dictionaries, however the IDEA behind the word certainly was present at Pearl Harbor that year. Newer dictionaries define "survivalist" as a person "who views survival of a catastrophic event as a primary objective."

Sixty years ago the adrenaline worked overtime in your bodies while the will to live worked overtime in your minds. The primary objective was to stay alive while surrounded by death. I believe you became survivalists on that fateful Sunday morning. In the years since then, it is likely that you have summoned that survivalist instinct in situations that will not make history books but have made you stronger people.

Some have survived the loss of loved ones — the loss of a job — the loss of property — the loss of money — the loss of health — or other things we deem important. But despite the losses, most of you have survived things like anger, anxiety, depression, fear or loneliness. You have even survived road rage on America's highways. CONGRATU-LATIONS!

In December 1941, I was a first grader at Central River-side school in Jacksonville, Florida. On Sunday afternoon, December 7, our family returned from a church service to hear radio bulletins about a Japanese air attack on U.S. Navy ships in Hawaii.

Soon my father was drafted into the Navy and served at Jacksonville Naval Air Station during World War II. Dad was on the flight line fueling Corsairs, PBYs and other air-craft.

While Dad was serving Uncle Same one way, I was do-ing my little patriotic part for the war effort, also. While soldiers and sailors did their thing around the world, my classmates and I were busy on the home front stomping on tin cans so that the flattened metal could be more easily re-cycled into making bayonets and bullets and tanks and planes. We were proud to save tinfoil and to buy U.S. savings stamps. At school there were posters that made us kids feel like we were helping win the war.

In the 40s it was politically correct to hate people. We school children were taught to hate "Japs" and "Krauts." In my mind's eye I can still see the grotesque caricatures of Japanese soldiers with the not-so-subtle captions that moti-vated young minds to hate yellow-skinned enemies. It took me many years to survive (overcome) that animosity and understand the wisdom of "love your enemies." For instance, as a young man after the war I had difficulty accepting the conversion story of Mitsuo Fuchida — the Japanese pilot who led the air assault on Pearl Harbor. It was reported that after the war Fuchida repented and became an active Christian.

My war-time hero was another pilot: USAF Colonel Robert Scott of "The Flying Tigers." After WWII, I was excited to hear Col. Scott speak in Jacksonville, and I also read his book, *God is My Co-Pilot*. A movie with the same title was one of my favorite flicks, and I wish I could see it again. I wonder what the scene was like in Heaven when Col. Scott met Fuchida for the first time.

Both airmen survived a horrible war in which they were military opponents. More significantly, I believe they survived mutual prejudice. I believe they also survived animosity toward the other man's country and its government.

About 15 years after the end of WWII, I had a close encounter with a former foe.

A German Luftwaffe pilot was the speaker at a service club luncheon I attended in Cincinnati, Ohio. He, like Fuchida, had experienced a post-war conversion to Christ, and that was his speech topic. I don't remember the speaker's name — but I'll never forget a faithful testimony that was clear through a German accent. I was so impressed with the pilot's sincereity and so curious to learn more that I offered to drive him back to the hotel where he was staying. In Cincinnati's traffic I discovered a warrior who had survived more than Allied ack-ack. He survived misinformation about the United States and misdirection by a madman named Hitler. Meanwhile the Luftwaffe officer helped me survive the bias against Germans I was taught back in grammar school.

I still perfer American cars to German cars, thank you, but in 1989, I gave may daughter's hand in marriage to a fine young man named Gatz, whose father was born in Germany.

Fifty years ago I shot imaginary guns at make-believe Germans on a Jacksonville playground. Today I play with grandchildren of German ancestry.

While memories of the second world war serve to make Americans diligent against alien agression, the prejudices, ill-will and hostility from that conflict must not survive into the 21st century. Certainly we can continue to learn from the past and avoid a repetition of military and political mistakes. But if the United States is to survive as a decent and civilized society, individual citizens must make the survival of spirit a top priority.

From a Boy Scout Handbook I learned, "Always be prepared." That helps me be a survivalist in human terms. From the Bible I learned, "Treat other people exactly as you would like to be treated by them." That helps me be a survivalist in spiritual terms.

There is no question that Pearl Harbor survivors ARE survivalists in human terms. That's what we celebrate for a while. I pray you may also be survivors in the spiritual dimension. That's something we can celebrate forever.

Survival situations vary. Let's consider three possibilities.

First, some people survive situations over which they have no control. We witnessed that in the Oklahoma City bombing.

Second, some people survive situations over which they have limited control. Air Force pilot Scott O'Brady is a recent model of this kind of survival

Third, some people survive situations over which they have complete control. A person who makes an informed decision to deliberately defy gravity must be prepared to experience the consequences of that decision.

The Bible teaches that we humans were created in the image of the triume God. We exist as body, soul and spirit. We function in three dimensions: physical, mental and spiritual. In an individual's lifetime he is challenged to be a survivalist in all three areas.

I may have limited control over my physical and mental survivability, but I have complete control my spiritual destiny. I am free to make moral and spiritual decisions as long as my body and mind survive.

The Old Testament character Job was the quintessential survivalist. Job suffered the loss of wealth, health and family. He suffered ridicule from his wife and bad advice from his friends. Job survived the devil's attacks, and in the last chapter of the book that bears his name we read, "The Lord restored Job's losses," and "the Lord blessed, the latter days of Job more than his beginning."

Survivalists never lose hope. They don't just survive, they thrive — especially when their lives are linked to Jesus who said, "I am come that they may have life, and that they may have it more abundantly."

Happy is he who, in the twilight years of life, is survivng and thriving.

I wish that for each of you.

I closing this book, I share with you a prayer from your former Commander-in-Chief. Most Americans recall President Franklin Roosevelt's description of December 7, 1941, as "a date which will live in infamy." How many remember his D-Day prayer? While allied troops were landing on the French coast, President Roosevelt wrote a prayer, and later that day he read it to the nation on a network radio broadcast. Here is condensed version of FDR's prayer.

Almighty God: Our sons, pride of our nation, this day have set upon a mighty endeavor, a struggle to preserve our Republic, our religion and our civilization, and to set free a suffering humanity. Lead them straight and true; give strength to their arms, stoutness to their hearts, steadfastness in their faith. . . . And, O Lord, give us faith: give us faith in Thee; faith in our sons; faith in each other; faith in our united crusade. Let not the keenness of our spirit ever be dulled. . . . With Thy blessing we shall prevail over the unholy forces of our enemy. Help us to conquer the apostles of greed and racial arrogances. Lead us to the saving of our country, and with our sister nations into a world unity that will spell a sure peace — a peace invulnerable to the scheming of unworthy men. And a peace that will let all men live in freedom, reaping the just rewards of their honest toil. Thy will be done, Almighty God. Amen.

A young Dick Jensen with his father, Kenneth and his sister, Joan, at Jacksonville, Florida in 1943 *(photo by Marguerite Jensen).*

Epilogue

September 11, 2001 is another date that will live in infamy. On that Tuesday morning more that 5,000 people died in New York, Pennsylvania and Virginia as a result of terrorist attacks.

In less that one hour, four hijacked U.S. commercial jetliners were deliberately crashed into the Pentagon, the World Trade Center's skyscrapers in Manhattan, and a rural site south of Pittsburgh.

As this book was going to press government agencies were trying to determine who was responsible for this evil conspiracy against the USA. Unlike the 1941 response to a known enemy, there was no immediate formal declaration of war from the U.S. Congress. President George W. Bush made it clear, however, that he considered the coordinated attacks to be the product of international terrorists based in the Middle East. The promised retaliation by the United States and its allies was pending as this book was being printed.

If the purpose of the 2001 attack was to demoralize Americans, the enemies of freedom failed again as they did at Pearl Harbor. Americans are united now in a spirit of patriotism and prayer not witnessed since December, 1941. Our symbloic eagle not only survives — it continues to soar!

"But they that wait upon the Lord shall renew their strength; they shall mount up with wings as eagles...."
Isaiah 40:31

Anchor from USS ARIZONA at the memorial in Pearl Harbor *(photo by Richard Sawyer).*

Appendix A

Ships Present at Pearl Harbor, 0800 7 December 1941

The U.S. Navy ships in list below are sorted by type and hull number, for example *New Orleans* (CA-32) is found in hull number order under heavy cruisers. For the purposes of this list, yard craft assigned to the Fourteenth Naval District and other small non-commissioned craft are not included. In addition, Pearl Harbor is defined as the area inside the nets guarding the harbor entrance.

Ships marked with an asterisk (*) were within twelve miles of the island of Oahu but were not actually within Pearl Harbor as defined above. Locations of these ships are indicated. Ships marked with a number symbol (#) were sunk or destroyed during the Pearl Harbor attack. All of these were later raised and rebuilt except for *Arizona, Oklahoma,* and *Utah. Oklahoma* was raised but not rebuilt.

Battleships (BB)

	Pennsylvania	(BB-38)	(in drydock)
#	Arizona	(BB-39)	
	Nevada	(BB-36)	
#	Oklahoma	(BB-37)	
	Tennessee	(BB-43)	
#	California	(BB-44)	
	Maryland	(BB-46)	
#	West Virginia	(BB-48)	

Heavy Cruisers (CA)

New Orleans	(CA-32)
San Francisco	(CA-38)

Light Cruisers (CL)

Raleigh	(CL-7)
Detroit	(CL-8)
Phoenix	(CL-46)
Honolulu	(CL-48)
St. Louis	(CL-49)
Helena	(CL-50)

Destroyers (DD)

	Allen	(DD-66)	
	Schley	(DD-103)	
	Chew	(DD-106)	
*	Ward	(DD-139)	(Patrolling Channel Entrance to Pearl Harbor)
	Dewey	(DD-349)	
	Farragut	(DD-348)	
	Hull	(DD-350)	
	MacDonough	(DD-351)	
	Worden	(DD-352)	
	Dale	(DD-353)	
	Monaghan	(DD-354)	
	Aylwin	(DD-355)	
	Selfridge	(DD-357)	
	Phelps	(DD-360)	

Cummings	(DD-365)	
Reid	(DD-369)	
Case	(DD-370)	
Conyngham	(DD-371)	
Cassin	(DD-372)	(In Drydock)
Shaw	(DD-373)	(In Floating Drydock)
Tucker	(DD-374)	
Downes	(DD-375)	(In Drydock)
Bagley	(DD-386)	
Blue	(DD-387)	
Helm	(DD-388)	
Mugford	(DD-389)	
Ralph Talbot	(DD-390)	
Henley	(DD-391)	
Patterson	(DD-392)	
Jarvis	(DD-393)	

Submarines (SS)

Narwhat	(SS-167)
Dolphin	(SS-169)
Cachalot	(SS-170)
Tautog	(SS-199)

Minelayer (CM)

#	Oglala	(CM-4)

Minesweeper (AM)

Turkey	(AM-13)
Bobolink	(AM-20)
Rail	(AM-26)
Tern	(AM-31)
Grebe	(AM-43)
Vireo	(AM-52)

Coastal Minsweeper (Amc)

Cockatoo	(Amc-8)
Crossbill	(Amc-9)
Condor	(Amc-14)
Reedbird	(Amc-30)

Destroyer Minelayer (DM)
Gamble	(DM-15)
Ramsay	(DM-16)
Montgomery	(DM-17)
Breese	(DM-18)
Tracy	(DM-19)
Preble	(DM-20)
Sicard	(DM-21)
Pruitt	(DM-22)

Destroyer Minesweeper (DMS)
Zane	(DMS-14)
Wasmuth	(DMS-15)
Trever	(DMS-16)
Perry	(DMS-17)

Patrol Gunboat (PG)
Sacramento	(PG-19)

Destroyer Tender (AD)
Dobbin	(AD-3)
Whitney	(AD-4)

Seaplane Tender (AV)
Curtiss	(AV-4)
Tangier	(AV-8)

Small Seaplane Tender (AVP)
Avocet	(AVP-4)	
Swan	(AVP-7)	(On Marine Railway Dock)

Ammunition Ship (AE)
Pyro	(AE-1)

Oiler (AO)
Ramapo	(AO-12)
Neosho	(AO-23)

Repair Ship (AR)
      Medusa   (AR-1)
      Vestal   (AR-4)
      Rigel   (AR-11)

Submarine Tender (AS)
      Pelias   (AS-14)

Submarine Rescue Ship (ASR)
      Widgeon   (ASR-1)

Hospital Ship (AH)
      Solace   (AH-5)

Cargo Ship (AK)
    * Vega   (AK-17)   (At Honolulu)

Stores Issue Ship (AKS)
      Castor   (AKS-1)
    * Antares   (AKS-3)   (At Pearl Harbor
                                                  Entrance)

Ocean Tug (AT)
      Ontario   (AT-13)
      Sunnadin   (AT-28)
    * Keosanqua   (AT-38)   (At Pearl Harbor
                                                  Entrance)
    * Navajo   (AT-64) (12-Miles Outside Pearl
                                            Harbor Entrance)

Miscellaneous Auxiliary (AG)
    # Utah   (AG-16)
      Argonne   (AG-31)
      Sumner   (AG-32)

A marine rifle squad fires a volley over the bodies of men killed at
Naval Air Station Kanoehe Bay during the December 7 raid. The
burial ceremony was December 8 *(U.S. Navy photo).*

Appendix B

One Hundred Third Congress
of the
United States of America

Joint Resolution

Designating December 7 of each year as
National Pearl Harbor Remembrance Day.

Whereas, on December 7, 1941, the Imperial Japanese Navy and Air Force attacked units of the armed forces of the United States stationed at Pearl Harbor, Hawaii;

Whereas, more than 2,000 citizens of the United States were killed and more than 1,000 citizens of the United States were wounded in the attack on Pearl Harbor;

Whereas, the attack on Pearl Harbor marked the entry of the United States into World War II;

Whereas, the veterans of World War II and all other people of the United States commemorate December 7 in remembrance of the attack on Pearl Harbor; and

Whereas, commemoration of the attack on Pearl Harbor will instill in all people of the United States a greater understanding and appreciation of the selfless sacrifice of the individuals who served in the armed forces of the United States during World War II: Now, therefore, be it

Resolved by the Senate and House of Representatives of the United States of America in Congress assembled, That December 7 of each year is designated as National Pearl Harbor Remembrance Day and the President is authorized and requested —

(1) to issue annually a proclamation calling on the people of the United States to observe the day with appropriate ceremonies and activities; and

(2) to urge all Federal agencies, and interested organizations, groups, and individuals, to fly the flag of the United States at halfstaff each December 7 in honor of the individuals who died as a result of their service at Pearl Harbor.

About First Foundations, Inc.

In 1984, Dick Jensen conceptualized the three primary foundations of any society as family, religion, and government. His inspiration came from Psalm 11:3. In 1986, the concept was organized into a nonprofit corporation, First Foundations, Inc., which researches and reports on societal foundations.

First Foundations, Inc. is a non-membership organization governed by a board of directors who serve without compensation. First Foundations is recognized by the IRS as a 501(c)(3) charitable organization. The operating budget is supported by the tax-deductible donations of individuals and corporations. Government grants or loans are neither sought nor accepted.

Although based in South Carolina, FFI has a nationwide constituency and international interests. FFI is a nonpartisan, non-sectarian, project-oriented organization.

Board of Directors

Dick Jensen, President   Greenville, SC
Marty Jensen, Secretary   Greenville, SC
Ben Davis, Jr., Treasurer   Greenwood, SC
Bates Brown, Jr.   Memphis, TN
Wm. T. Brown   Columbia, SC
Hubert McCommon   Memphis, TN
Jim Stovall   Greenville, SC

First Foundations, Inc.
P.O. Box 991
Travelers Rest, SC 29690